A BUSINESS APPROACH TO STRAWBERRY FARMING

Complete Entrepreneurial Step By Step Guide To Strawberry Garden From Scratch

ZHURI HART

DISCLAIMER

This book is intended to provide general information and insights on adopting a business approach to farming. The content within is based on the author's knowledge and experiences up to the date of publication. It is essential to recognize that the field of agriculture is dynamic, influenced by various factors such as market conditions, climate, and regulatory changes.

Readers are advised to conduct thorough research, seek professional advice, and consider their unique circumstances before implementing any strategies or practices discussed in this book. The author and publisher disclaim any responsibility for the accuracy, completeness, or suitability of the information provided. The book is not a substitute for professional advice, and the author and publisher shall not be liable for any damages or losses arising from the use or reliance on the information presented herein.

Individual results may vary, and success in farming enterprises is contingent upon numerous variables. The author encourages readers to consult with relevant experts, agricultural extension services, and legal or financial professionals to tailor strategies to their specific needs and local conditions.

This book is not intended to be a comprehensive guide to all aspects of farming, and readers should exercise their judgment and discretion in applying the principles discussed. The author and publisher do not endorse any specific products, services, or companies mentioned in this book unless explicitly stated.

By reading this book, the reader acknowledges and accepts the inherent uncertainties in agricultural endeavors and agrees to use the information at their own risk.

TABLE OF CONTENTS

ABOUT THE BOOK

For those wishing to enter the strawberry farming industry from a strategic and business-oriented standpoint, the book "A Business Approach to Strawberry Farming" provides an extensive manual. By exploring the backdrop of strawberry cultivation and throwing light on its historical context and evolution, the introductory portion offers a strong foundation. The importance of using a business strategy is emphasized, along with the necessity of an organized and structured methodology in this agricultural industry.

"Understanding the Strawberry Market," readers can better understand consumer wants, market dynamics, and trends. Farmers need to know this information to stay competitive, make wise decisions, and match their output to the always-shifting demands of their customers. Incorporating competition analysis guarantees farmers are adequately equipped to properly navigate the market landscape.

"Setting Up Your Strawberry Farm," helpful advice is given on crucial topics including choosing a suitable location, preparing the soil, and choosing strawberry varieties. The part also covers planting and propagation methods, giving readers the know-how they need to start a profitable strawberry farm.

"Farm Management and Best Practices," provides a thorough examination of important topics such as pest management, soil fertility, irrigation, and sustainable agricultural methods. These subjects complement the overall business-oriented approach of the book and are essential to preserving crop health and maximizing yield.

"Business Planning and Strategy," which follows, explores the strategic facets of strawberry farming. The process of drafting a thorough business plan, budgeting, risk management, and financial projections is walked readers through. The necessity of placing the strawberry farm into the larger market is highlighted by the inclusion of marketing and sales techniques.

"Harvesting and Post-Harvest Handling," the best methods for harvesting, packing, storing, and shipping are covered in detail. By doing this, the produce's marketability and profitability are increased and its quality is maintained from the farm to the market.

"Technology and Innovation in Strawberry Farming," information technology integration for farm management, precision agriculture, and contemporary agricultural technologies are examined. This forward-looking viewpoint guarantees that readers are informed about the most recent developments that can improve production and efficiency in strawberry cultivation.

"Case Studies and Success Stories," provides practical illustrations of prosperous strawberry farms to enhance the reader's comprehension. These case studies are an invaluable tool for readers to gain knowledge from the experiences of others in the field since they provide real-world perspectives, lessons discovered, and best practices from successful businesses. Overall, "A Business Approach to Strawberry Farming" is a thorough manual that instills a strategic mentality for success in the ever-changing industry of strawberry farming in addition to imparting technical knowledge.

CHAPTER ONE

INTRODUCTION TO STRAWBERRY FARMING

HISTORY OF STRAWBERRY PRODUCTION

Within the field of agriculture, strawberry cultivation is particularly interesting and profitable. The history of strawberry farming begins with the cultivation of the genus Fragaria, which is a species of flowering plant that yields the delicious, vivid red fruit that we all know and love as strawberries.

Since they first appeared in Europe centuries ago, these berries have traveled across continents, adjusting to a variety of conditions and rising in popularity as a commodity around the world.

The background of strawberry farming history shows a slow transition from foraging for berries in the wild to intentional production. Strawberries were first harvested from the wild, and little was done in the way of cultivation.

But when farmers started methodically growing these delicious berries due to the increasing demand, specific methods and types were created. With this development, strawberry cultivation went from being a subsistence endeavor to a profitable business.

THE VALUE OF A BUSINESS STRATEGY

It is impossible to exaggerate the significance of using a business strategy when growing strawberries. Although growing a tasty fruit has inherent appeal, approaching strawberry farming as a company highlights the necessity of financial management, market research, and strategic planning. Farmers who adopt a business-oriented mindset can turn what would otherwise be a hobby or traditional practice into a profitable and sustainable enterprise by seeing their operations through these two lenses.

Numerous advantages result from the commercialization of strawberry cultivation for both individual growers and the overall economy.

Farmers may improve resource use, develop effective farming practices, and adjust to market demands by adopting a commercial perspective. This helps to stabilize and expand the agricultural industry in addition to increasing the strawberry farm's overall output.

Moreover, the commercial strategy for growing strawberries is in line with customer tastes and the current dynamics of international trade. Strawberries are now cultivated far beyond local markets to meet global demand, as they have become a mainstay in many culinary delicacies. Farmers can access these larger markets by using a strategic business approach, which promotes economic growth on both the local and national levels.

The history of growing the Fragaria genus—from wild berries to carefully cultivated crops—is what gives rise to the practice of strawberry farming. The economic potential and commercial value of strawberry cultivation are acknowledged by highlighting the significance of a business strategy in this undertaking. Strawberry farming is transformed into a vibrant industry that contributes to the global agricultural landscape, in addition to being a source of delicious berries, by combining conventional agricultural techniques with market-oriented strategies and strategic planning.

CHAPTER TWO

COMPREHENDING THE STRAWBERRY INDUSTRY

INDUSTRY TRENDS AND DEMAND

A variety of factors impact the strawberry industry, which is prone to dynamic trends and shifting demand. The increasing knowledge and inclination of consumers for natural and healthful food options is one notable development over the past few years. Due to their high antioxidant, vitamin, and mineral content, strawberries have become a popular option for health-conscious consumers.

The growing market for fresh strawberries and items made with strawberries reflects this tendency. Furthermore, a change in consumer behavior has been brought about by the trend towards locally sourced and sustainable produce, which has increased demand for strawberries that come from organic or locally obtained sources.

The rising appeal of quick meals and snacks is a key factor influencing the strawberry market. Demand for processed strawberry products—such as jams, preserves, and frozen strawberries—that provide convenience without sacrificing flavor or nutritional content is growing as people lead busier lives. To meet the need for strawberry products that are simple to use and save time, the strawberry processing industry is experiencing a shift in customer behavior that is pushing innovation.

COMPETITIVE ANALYSIS

Many companies are fighting for market share in the strawberry industry, which is characterized by fierce competition. Given that fresh strawberries are a seasonal product, being able to guarantee a year-round supply is one of the primary factors determining success in the market. Large-scale commercial strawberry farms frequently enjoy a competitive edge due to their capacity for distribution and economies of scale.

On the other hand, local, smaller producers could be able to carve out a niche by focusing on things like direct-to-consumer sales, unusual varietals, or organic farming methods.

An important factor in the competitive environment of the strawberry market is international trade. Major exporters of strawberries include the United States, Mexico, and Spain, all of which have climates that are suitable for growing strawberries. This creates a complex web of competition between these countries. Furthermore, by improving yield and quality, technological innovations like precision farming and controlled-environment agriculture boost the competitiveness of different market participants.

CUSTOMER PREFERENCES

Success in the strawberry industry requires a thorough understanding of customer preferences. When it comes to fresh strawberries, consumers are influenced by several aspects, including taste, freshness, and aesthetic appeal. Customers frequently favor strawberries that are juicy, sweet, and have a bright color. To meet these expectations and guarantee that strawberries reach consumers in ideal form, care must be taken during cultivation, harvesting, and post-harvest processing.

Consumer preferences for processed strawberry goods also include things like texture, sweetness levels, and the lack of artificial ingredients. Customers who are concerned about their health could look for goods that are branded as organic and pesticide-free or with a lower sugar content. Innovative strawberry-based goods that satisfy a range of dietary requirements, such as gluten-free, vegan, and non-GMO choices, are also becoming more and more popular.

All things considered, all parties involved in the strawberry industry must be aware of changing consumer preferences, be they those related to convenience, sustainability, or health conscience.

CHAPTER THREE

ESTABLISHING A STRAWBERRY FARM

CHOOSING A SITE AND PREPARING THE SOIL

The success of your strawberry farm depends on your decision on the location of the farm. Choose a location that receives adequate sunlight, preferably six to eight hours a day. The ideal soil has a pH of between 5.5 and 6.5, is rich in organic content, and drains well. Test the soil to ascertain its composition and apply any necessary amendments, such as pH adjustments or the addition of organic matter. To avoid waterlogging, which can be harmful to strawberry plants, proper drainage is necessary.

After choosing a good location, thoroughly prepare the soil. Clear away any garbage, rocks, or weeds that might impede the growth of plants. Dig a 6-to 8-inch hole in the dirt to generate a loose, well-aerated growing medium. To enhance soil fertility and structure, add organic matter, such as compost or well-rotted manure.

This preparation guarantees that the soil offers the best possible circumstances for the establishment and uptake of vital nutrients by strawberry roots.

SELECTING TYPES OF STRAWBERRIES

Choosing the right strawberry cultivars is a crucial choice that affects your farm's profitability. Take into consideration elements like the intended usage of the berries, the local weather, and the climate. Strawberries come in three primary varieties: day-neutral, everbearing, and June-bearing.

June-bearing cultivars yield a solitary, substantial crop in late spring or early summer. Two crops are usually produced by everbearing varieties: one in the spring and another in the late summer or early fall. Day-neutral varieties can produce fruit all during the growing season. Select cultivars that are compatible with the climate and temperature swings in your area.

Take into account the berries' hardness, flavor, and size as well, as these qualities can change throughout types. To learn more about the best strawberry varieties for your particular location and market demands, speak with knowledgeable farmers, nurseries, or agricultural extension organizations in your area.

TECHNIQUES FOR PLANTING AND PROPAGATION

The timing and methods employed when planting strawberries are critical to the crop's establishment and productivity. Most commonly, runners, bare-root plants, or tissue-cultured plants are used to propagate strawberry plants.

Little plantlets known as runners are produced by the parent plant and can be planted to create new plants.

Depending on the variety and local climate, planting should take place in the early spring or late summer. Plants should be spaced in rows of three to four feet apart, often 12 to 18 inches apart, per the instructions. When planting, make sure the roots are evenly distributed in the planting hole and the plant's crown is at the soil level.

In particular, throughout the flowering and fruiting seasons, maintain uniform moisture levels by putting in place an appropriate irrigation system. Mulching the area around the plants aids in temperature regulation, moisture retention, and weed suppression.

Strawberries are vulnerable to several problems, so keep an eye out for and take appropriate action against pests and illnesses. Biological, cultural, and chemical control techniques are all combined in integrated pest management (IPM) approaches, which can help guarantee a robust and fruitful strawberry harvest.

You can start a profitable and productive strawberry farm by being mindful of site selection, soil preparation, variety selection, planting, and propagation methods. Every action you take improves the general well-being and output of your strawberry plants, resulting in a bumper crop and a long-lasting agricultural enterprise.

CHAPTER FOUR

AGRICULTURAL ADMINISTRATION AND OPTIMAL TECHNIQUES

MANAGEMENT OF WATER AND IRRIGATION

Effective water and irrigation management are essential elements of productive farm management. Using water resources wisely is crucial to maximize crop yields and reduce waste. To make sure that crops receive the proper amount of water at the right time, farmers use a variety of irrigation techniques, including furrow irrigation, sprinkler systems, and drip irrigation. By supplying water straight to the root zone, drip irrigation, for cxample, lowers water loss from evaporation and runoff.

Monitoring soil moisture levels and modifying irrigation schedules accordingly are further components of proper water management. Modern technological innovations like soil moisture sensors and computerized irrigation systems have significantly increased the accuracy and effectiveness of farm water applications. Sustainable water management techniques can include the use of water-saving techniques like rainwater collection and irrigation runoff recycling.

FERTILITY OF SOILS AND MANAGEMENT OF NUTRIENTS

Sustaining agricultural productivity requires maintaining soil fertility. The ability of the soil to give plants the vital nutrients they need is referred to as soil fertility. Farmers use a variety of techniques, such as crop rotation, cover crops, and the addition of organic matter, to improve soil fertility. Compost and manure are examples of organic matter that enhances the nutritional content and soil structure, creating a favorable environment for plant growth.

The careful application of fertilizers by crop requirements and soil nutrient levels is known as nutrient management. An essential tool for managing nutrients in the soil is soil testing, which gives farmers information on the kind and quantity of fertilizers they need. Crop rotation, which involves planting various crops in a particular order, contributes to sustainable soil fertility management by lowering the risk of soil-borne illnesses and preventing nutrient depletion.

CONTROL OF PESTS AND DISEASES

Protecting crop health and optimizing production need effective pest and disease control. The comprehensive strategy known as Integrated Pest Management (IPM) blends chemical, cultural, and biological control techniques. While cultural measures like crop rotation and planting resistant types help avoid illness, biological management uses natural predators and parasites to control pest populations.

Pest management includes chemical control, which includes the use of pesticides, although it is done so carefully to reduce its negative effects on the environment. Farmers may stop problems from getting worse by keeping an eye out for symptoms of pests and illnesses on their crops. This allows them to take prompt action. Using IPM techniques helps the farming ecosystem maintain ecological balance while lowering dependency on chemical inputs.

ROTATING CROPS AND SUSTAINABLE METHODS

A key component of sustainable farming is crop rotation, which entails planting various crops on the same plot of land in a particular order. This method strengthens soil structure, promotes nutrient cycling, and breaks the cycles of disease and pests. Farmers can maintain overall soil fertility and stop the depletion of individual nutrients by rotating crops with varying nutrient demands.

Beyond crop rotation, sustainable farming methods include a comprehensive approach to land management. Agroforestry, cover crops, and conservation tillage are a few examples of techniques that reduce soil erosion, increase biodiversity, and support long-term environmental sustainability.

The use of GPS-guided equipment and other precision agriculture technologies reduces waste and environmental impact by enabling more accurate resource usage.

Effective farm management necessitates a thorough comprehension and application of soil fertility and nutrient management, irrigation and water management, disease and insect control, and sustainable methods like crop rotation. By incorporating these ideas into a well-thought-out farming plan, agricultural systems are guaranteed to be resilient and viable for the long run in addition to maximizing present yields.

CHAPTER FIVE

PLANNING AND STRATEGY FOR BUSINESSES

MAKING A BUSINESS STRATEGY

A well-written business plan offers a path for a company's growth and development, acting as the blueprint for its success. It includes several components, including the mission, vision, goals, and strategies of the organization. Market, competitor, and target audience analyses are usually included in a thorough business strategy. It provides an overview of the operational procedures, product or service offers, and organizational structure.

A well-written business plan not only directs the company's internal operations but also plays a vital role in securing funds or forming alliances. Developing a business plan necessitates careful consideration, analytical reasoning, and strategic planning to guarantee a strong basis for the enterprise.

BUDGETS AND FINANCIAL PROJECTIONS

Budgeting and financial estimates are essential elements of successful company planning. Financial projections entail projecting the company's future financial performance using market trends, historical data, and other pertinent information.

This involves projecting earnings, costs, and profits for a given time frame. On the other hand, budgeting entails developing a thorough plan for distributing resources among the several tasks carried out by the company.

A well-crafted budget facilitates cash flow management, the identification of possible financial obstacles, and well-informed decision-making. Financial predictions and budgeting serve as a foundation for evaluating performance versus objectives and making required modifications, which both support the business's overall financial health and sustainability.

RISK MANAGEMENT

In today's fast-paced business world, risk management is essential to averting possible dangers and guaranteeing the company's long-term survival. A thorough risk management plan includes locating, evaluating, and ranking risks that might influence the accomplishment of corporate goals. These risks could include shifts in the market, modifications to regulations, difficulties in running the business, and external economic variables. A business can take proactive steps to reduce risks and create backup plans in case of unanticipated events by being aware of potential risks. A strong framework for risk management not only protects the company but also promotes resilience and adaptation by enabling quick decisions in the face of shifting conditions.

STRATEGIES FOR MARKETING AND SALES

A business plan's marketing and sales strategies are crucial for generating money and assisting with customer acquisition and retention. A product or service's marketing efforts include raising awareness of it and building demand for it, whereas sales is the process of turning leads into paying clients. Target audiences are identified, several channels are used, and a strong value proposition is communicated in a successful marketing plan. Contrarily, sales methods emphasize relationship-building, comprehending client demands, and closing transactions. By combining these tactics, one can guarantee a unified strategy for drawing in and keeping clients, which eventually helps the company succeed and expand. To remain competitive in ever-changing markets, these methods must be regularly assessed and adjusted.

CHAPTER SIX

HARVESTING AND HANDLING AFTER HARVEST

THE BEST HARVESTING METHODS

Ensuring the quality and yield of agricultural output is contingent upon the implementation of optimal harvesting techniques. Harvesting at the right time of year has a significant influence on the nutritional value, flavor, and general quality of the harvested crops.

To decide the best time for harvesting, farmers must take into account the crop's unique requirements, weather, and maturation stage. Harvesting produce at the ideal stage of maturity guarantees optimal flavor and nutritional content.

To minimize damage to the crops, harvesting techniques are just as important as timing. Produce bruising and other physical damage can be avoided by using the right tools and gentle handling techniques. Harvesters that are mechanized are examples of modern technology that can increase productivity without sacrificing the quality of the crop. To maximize output and quality, only fully grown crops should be harvested, a practice known as selective harvesting.

The post-harvest process includes packaging and storage, which have a significant impact on the durability and marketability of agricultural products. Crops that are packaged properly are shielded from degradation, microbiological contamination, and physical harm.

The produce's unique qualities and the length of time it will be stored determine which packing material is best. Breathable packaging may be necessary for perishable goods to regulate moisture levels and lower the chance of mildew or rot.

Storage facilities are made to keep various crop varieties in the best possible conditions. Carefully controlled variables including temperature, humidity, and ventilation help to prolong the shelf life of harvested produce.

Fruits and vegetables are frequently kept in cold storage to delay ripening and maintain freshness. The capacity to customize storage conditions for individual crops is made possible by advancements in controlled environment storage, which guarantee low nutrient loss and extended quality.

DISTRIBUTION AND TRANSPORTATION

The timely delivery of agricultural products from farms to customers while preserving their quality and freshness depends on effective distribution and transportation. The kind of food, the distance to be traveled, and the crops' time sensitivity all influence the mode of transportation. Transporting perishable items needs to be done in a refrigerator to keep them from spoiling while en route. The quality of fruits, vegetables, and other temperature-sensitive items must be preserved along the cold chain, which entails keeping a constant low temperature from harvest to consumption.

Another crucial aspect of shipping is proper handling. Produce damage can be avoided by using secure packing and being careful when loading and unloading. To minimize transit times and lower the possibility of delays that could compromise product quality, distribution networks must be well-organized. Technology integration, such as real-time tracking systems, improves supply chain visibility and control and guarantees that goods arrive at their destination in ideal condition. Efficient transportation and distribution networks facilitate the timely and efficient connection between farmers and consumers, hence augmenting the overall prosperity of the agricultural value chain.

CHAPTER SEVEN

INNOVATION AND TECHNOLOGY IN STRAWBERRY FARMING

CONTEMPORARY AGRICULTURE TECHNOLOGIES

The field of strawberry farming has seen tremendous change as a result of modern farming technologies, bringing in a period of increased productivity, sustainability, and efficiency. One noteworthy technological advancement is the use of sophisticated irrigation, harvesting, and planting machines. By ensuring accurate and consistent spacing, automated planters maximize the use of available resources and land. Furthermore, robotic harvesting devices with computer vision systems improve the efficiency and precision of selecting ripe strawberries, saving labor expenses and cutting down on waste.

In strawberry farming, the application of data analytics has created new opportunities for production optimization.

To create prediction models, machine learning algorithms examine past data on crop production, pest infestations, and weather trends. These models help farmers foresee problems so that preemptive steps can be taken. Predictive analytics, for instance, can assist farmers in modifying irrigation schedules in response to impending weather or putting preventative measures in place to deal with possible pest outbreaks, thereby enhancing crop health and production in general.

ACCURATE FARMING

In strawberry farming, precision agriculture has become a game-changer by providing a data-driven method of decision-making. This technique gathers data on crop health, weather patterns, and soil conditions in real-time using sensors, GPS, and other cutting-edge equipment. Farmers can make well-informed decisions on pest control, fertilization, and irrigation by examining this data. By conserving resources and lowering the need for chemical inputs, precision agriculture not only maximizes productivity but also reduces its negative effects on the environment.

Drones are being used for surveillance and monitoring in strawberry farms. Drones with high-resolution cameras and sensors can take precise pictures of the whole field. This information can be used to evaluate the health of the plants, spot diseased or stressed areas, and improve irrigation techniques. Farmers can examine broad regions quickly and affordably with the use of drones, enabling them to take prompt action and make judgments.

IT INTEGRATION FOR FARM MANAGEMENT

For contemporary strawberry growers, integrating information technology (IT) with farm management has become essential. Efficient planning, monitoring, and analysis of several parts of the farming operation are made possible by farm management software. This covers financial analysis, labor tracking, and inventory management. Cloud-based technologies make it possible for farmers to oversee and make decisions remotely by giving them access to vital information from any location. Furthermore, a complete solution for holistic farm management is offered by the integration of IT systems with precision agriculture technologies, encouraging sustainability and adaptability in the face of changing circumstances.

The strawberry farm's numerous gadgets and sensors are now connected thanks in large part to the Internet of Things (IT). IoT networks can facilitate communication between soil moisture sensors, weather stations, and individual plant sensors.

Real-time insights into the farm's conditions are provided by this networked system, which enables farmers to make quick modifications to maximize resource use. The integration of intelligent irrigation systems that can be remotely managed using information gathered from field sensors is made easier by the Internet of Things.

Strawberry farming has undergone a revolution thanks to the combination of cutting-edge farming technologies, precision agriculture, and IT for farm management. These developments reduce resource consumption and environmental effects while simultaneously increasing production and efficiency. Farmers that grow strawberries should anticipate more technological advancements that will influence this important agricultural industry going forward.

CHAPTER EIGHT

CASE STUDIES AND TRIUMPHANT NARRATIVES

EXAMPLES OF SUCCESSFUL STRAWBERRY FARMS IN THE REAL WORLD

The success stories of strawberry farms provide insightful case studies in a variety of agricultural contexts, illuminating the nuances of cultivation, innovation, and sustainable methods. The Frais Berry Farm, located in the center of California, is one such excellent model. By utilizing cutting-edge technologies like precision agriculture and vertical farming, this farm has set itself apart.

Frais Berry Farm uses sensor technologies and data analytics to monitor soil conditions, adjust irrigation, and make sure every strawberry plant gets the exact nutrients it needs to grow strong.

This technological integration has demonstrated the potential for efficiency and sustainability in contemporary strawberry farming by increasing output while reducing resource consumption.

The Sweet Harvest Cooperative in Spain is another noteworthy example of success. The cooperation of the nearby strawberry farmers has allowed this cooperative to flourish.

By pooling resources, exchanging knowledge, and coordinating marketing initiatives, the cooperative has established a robust and mutually advantageous ecosystem.

This concept highlights how crucial community involvement and cooperation are to the prosperity of strawberry-growing endeavors. The Sweet Harvest Co-operatives farmers have enhanced their collective bargaining power in the market, negotiated better pricing, and invested in shared infrastructure by pooling their resources, which has eventually increased profitability for all members.

BEST PRACTICES AND LESSONS LEARNED

Strawberry farm success stories can teach existing agricultural firms and prospective farmers alike important lessons and best practices. The importance of implementing ecologically friendly and sustainable methods is one important lesson.

Organic farming practices are given priority to productive strawberry farms, with minimal usage of artificial fertilizers and pesticides. In addition to making produce healthier, this also fits with consumers' increasing desires for food goods that are supplied ethically and sustainably.

Furthermore, diversification becomes apparent as an essential tactic for reducing risks and optimizing earnings in the strawberry industry. An exemplary case in point is the Berry Patch Farm located in Canada. The farm has established several revenue streams by broadening its product line to include processed goods like jams and juices in addition to fresh strawberries.

This strategy contributes to the long-term stability of the company by mitigating the effects of seasonal and market changes.

In addition, adopting new technologies is crucial to maintaining a competitive edge in the strawberry growing sector. Productivity is increased by the use of automated harvesting machinery, data-driven decision-making procedures, and precision agriculture instruments. Effective integration of these technologies by farms can improve resource usage, cut waste, and streamline operations—all of which eventually increase yields and profitability.

The success stories of strawberry farms emphasize the value of an all-encompassing strategy that includes community involvement, sustainable practices, technological innovation, and diversification. These tips and tricks are a great resource for anyone hoping to grow this popular fruit successfully, as the farming environment is always changing.

www.ingramcontent.com/pod-product-compliance
Lightning Source LLC
Chambersburg PA
CBHW070840290526
45795CB00002B/925